Welcome

The art activities in the *Art Therapy Card Deck* are designed to help your challenging clients explore mastery, self-concept, and self-worth through art to assist in your therapeutic intervention.

Sometimes words aren't enough. Art therapy allows for processing and externalization of emotions, exploration of choices, and reflection on conflicts. This deck can help children and adolescents to develop a growth mindset, increase their frustration tolerance, and strengthen their communication skills to reach their goals.

How To Use This Deck

Select a few cards directed towards your client's needs and discuss which activities they would like to explore. You can adapt the cards to their individualized abilities or functioning level.

The cards were designed to assist children and adolescents who have:

- Anxiety
- Trauma
- Mood Disorders
- ODD (Oppositional Defiant Disorder)
- ASD (Autism Spectrum Disorder)
- ADHD (Attention Deficit Hyperactivity Disorder)

They are color-coded and each color represents a different core issue. Each card also features a photo of a completed creation to serve as an example.

Categories

● **Safety**

● **Relationships & Connection**

● **Self-Esteem**

● **Responsibility**

● **Control**

Exploration Questions

Each card has questions to deepen the discovery process and encourage a discussion around the art created.

I find it best to start with general questions such as, "What did you create?" and "What were you feeling as you created this?" and then continue to the exploration questions which are specific to the project.

About The Materials

The basic materials you will need for these activities are: paper, scissors, glue, drawing supplies such as markers, colored pencils, crayons, and gel pens, decoupage medium (I prefer Modge Podge®), paint, and paintbrushes. Several projects also use air-dry or modeling clay (I prefer Model Magic®), clay tools (such as a sponge, wooden modeling tools, and wire tools), and embellishments (such as feathers, ribbon, beads, etc.).

Additional Note

Please be mindful that the use of therapeutic art activities needs to be introduced after assessment of your client's functioning level. Therapists are advised to introduce art directives in small increments and use client responses to guide risk assessment and effectiveness. The use of this card deck is distinctly different from a formal training in art therapy and does not imply that the user is an art therapist or that they can practice art therapy without proper credentials.

About The Author

Laura Dessauer, Ed.D, **ATR-BC,** is a board-certified art therapist with a doctoral degree in counseling psychology who has been working with families for more than 35 years in over 21 school districts. Dr. Dessauer's work has been included in *Parents magazine*, *eHow Parenting*, *YourTango*, *Fox News*, *PBS's This Emotional Life*, *Working Mother*, and *Psychology Today*.

Dr. Dessauer is passionate about helping families develop ways to confidently communicate and creatively connect. In her private practice, she specializes in working with children who shut down, melt down, and act out. She playfully blends cognitive behavioral skills, art-making, and creative problem-solving to help clients create individualized social, emotional, and behavioral interventions that "stick to their brain."

©2023 Laura Dessauer • All Rights Reserved.
Published by PESI Publishing & Media
ISBN: 9781683736967

Safety

Bird Nest

Materials: Modeling clay, clay tools, embellishments, glue, paint, paintbrushes.

Directions: Use the clay and tools to sculpt a bird's nest and a baby bird. Allow the clay to dry and then paint the nest and bird. After the paint has dried, use glue to add embellishments.

Exploration:

What does a baby bird need to feel safe and secure?

What do you need to feel safe and secure?

What if you had a nest, what would be in it?

Safety

A Chill Space

Materials: Paper, scissors, glue, magazines, drawing supplies.

Directions: On the paper, draw a picture of a place you'd like to hang out and chill in. Then use magazines to cut out words or images to add to your space and add embellishments.

Exploration:

What sensory things might be there; what might you smell, touch, taste, hear, or see in this space?

Would you invite someone into your chill space; if so, who?

When might you want to go and hang out in this chill space to relax and calm down?

Safety

Brave Collage

Materials: Paper, scissors, glue, magazines, drawing supplies.

Directions: Use magazines to cut out words or images that represent bravery and create a collage. You can also add embellishments or stickers.

Exploration:

Think of a time when you were brave; what were you doing and thinking?

What's a word or a symbol you can use to remind yourself you are brave when you are feeling scared or overwhelmed?

Where can you put your brave collage to remind yourself that you are courageous?

Safety

Force Field

Materials: Paper, drawing supplies, magazines, scissors, glue.

Directions:
Think about something that is upsetting or a worry. Now think about a force field: a shield of energy that protects you from things that are negative. Using the art materials, create an image of you surrounded by your force field. Add images and words of things that worry you outside of your force field.

Exploration:
What worries you?

How do you typically respond and does it make the situation better or worse?

If you had a force field to protect you when you are feeling upset, what might you be thinking, doing, or feeling?

Would it be helpful to act like you have a force field when you encounter something upsetting?

Safety

Protect Your Treasure

Materials: Box, paper, scissors, markers, pencil, paint, paintbrushes.

Directions: Paint your treasure box. Add things that you treasure inside of the box. You can also write or draw things you treasure onto slips of paper and add them too.

Exploration:

What things would you want to keep safe by locking them up in a treasure box?

Would you put people in your box; if so, who?

Would you add any feelings or thoughts to your treasure box; if yes, what would they be?

Would you put places in your treasure box; if yes, which places?

Safety

Safety Shield

Materials: Large paper, pencil, glue, tape, markers, embellishments, magazines, scissors, paint, paintbrushes.

Directions: Draw a large shield and then cut it out. Cut a long strip of paper and tape it on the back of the shield to make a handle. Decorate the shield with colors, words, or images that make you feel safe.

Exploration:

If the shield had magical powers, what would they be?

When would you need your shield?

Could the shield have helped you in the past when you were experiencing a challenging situation; if so, how?

What could you say or do in the future to help remind yourself that you have this shield protecting you?

Safety

Calming Collage

Materials: Paper, soft embellishments (feathers, fabric, or tissue paper), glue, markers.

Directions: Take the piece of paper and glue on soft embellishments and draw other calming things.

Exploration:

What colors, textures, and senses are calming for you?

How do you feel when you are engaging different senses?

What part of the collage could you imagine yourself being in, and why? When might you want to go to that spot?

Are there words or anything else you might add to this collage as a reminder to help you feel calmer?

Safety

Worry in a Box

Materials: Heart-shaped box, embellishments, slips of paper, markers, glue, paint, paintbrushes.

Directions: Paint or color your box and then add embellishments. On the slips of paper write or draw repetitive thoughts that you have and put them in the box.

Exploration:

What do you think about repeatedly?

Is this something you can change or not?

Can you think of the heart-shaped box and say the words "heart-shaped box" when you think of a repeated thought?

How might you feel knowing your worry is in a box and you don't need to keep it in your head?

Safety

Create a Monster

Materials: Paper, drawing supplies.

Directions: Think about something that scares you or upsets you. Create that worry, upset, or fear as a monster.

Exploration:

How big or little is that fear or upset in real life compared to the size of the monster drawing?

When does that monster show up?

Can we create something to help make that monster smaller, such as a helper, container, or other character?

What should we do with this monster drawing?

Relationship & Connections

Family Sculpture

Materials: Modeling clay, clay tools, embellishments, markers, glue, paint, paintbrushes.

Directions: Use the clay and tools to create representations of your family members. Allow the clay to dry, then paint or decorate your sculpture with markers. After the paint has dried, you can add embellishments.

Exploration:

What are your family members doing?

Does your family do these activities in real life or are these activities something you wished you could do?

Did you make a sculpture of everyone together or separately; why?

Who are you closest to in your family and why?

Relationship & Connections

All About Me Collage

Materials: Large paper, magazines, glue, scissors, drawing supplies.

Directions: Use magazine images, words, or drawings to create a collage of what is important to you. Think about what people, places, or things you value and add them to the collage.

Exploration:

What is important to you and why?

Who else knows what is important to you?

How often do you get to do, be with, or visit what is important to you?

What can you do so you have more opportunities to spend time with what you like?

Relationship & Connections

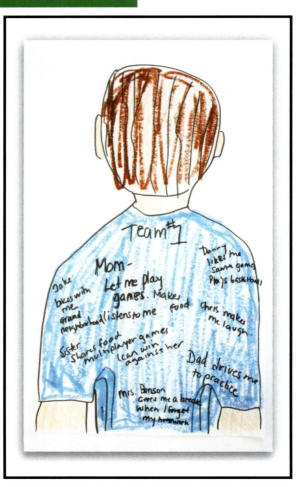

Got My Back

Materials: Large paper, drawing supplies, embellishments.

Directions: If you are comfortable, lie down on the paper and have someone trace your upper body. If you prefer not to be traced, you can draw a person's upper body: head, neck, shoulders, arms, and torso. When you are done creating the drawing add words or images on the picture to show the different ways you are supported and others have "got your back" or are there for you in good and bad times.

Exploration:

When you are struggling how do you get through it?

Who is there to help you through challenges?

What do they say or do that might be helpful and how does that feel?

Can you remind yourself of some of the things they say or do when you are feeling challenged?

Relationship & Connections

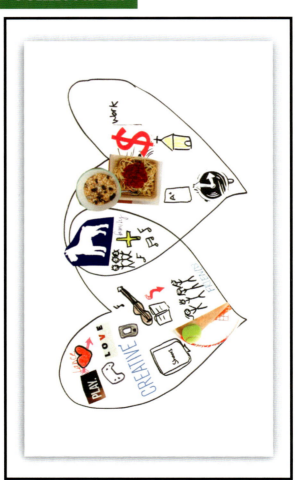

Two Hearts

Materials: Large paper, magazines, glue, scissors, drawing supplies.

Directions: Draw two large overlapping hearts that
fill the page. Think about what's important to you, like people, places, or things. In one heart, add words or images about what you value. In the other heart, add things that are important to the people that you love. In the middle where the hearts overlap, add words or images of things you have in common.

Exploration:

What's important to you and why is it in your heart?

How is it similar to or different from the other heart?

Can you spend time with the person you love doing or talking about what is in the middle?

Do you sometimes get into disagreements with the other person because you value different things?

Relationship & Connections

Walk in My Shoes

Materials: Shoe or pair of shoes, embellishments, paint, paintbrushes.

Directions: Think about what it is like to be uniquely you. Paint the shoe(s) and then add images or words that represent what's important to you. Add embellishments after the project is dry.

Exploration:

What are some experiences you have had that make you unique and special?

What are some challenges you've experienced?

Would you want to walk in someone else's shoes; if so, whose and why?

If someone had to walk in your shoes for a day, what kind of thoughts and feelings might they have?

Relationship & Connections

Water My Garden

Materials: Paper, drawing supplies, glitter glue, embellishments.

Directions: Draw a picture of a garden and different plants and flowers that represent important relationships in your life. If you like, add an image of yourself watering the garden. Write the names of the relationships and discuss how you can nurture and support them and how they support you.

Exploration:

Who is important to you?

When you are with these special people, how do you feel?

What do you need to do and say to help these relationships grow?

Relationship & Connections

What Is in Your Heart?

Materials: Fabric, needle, thread, polyester stuffing, small slips of paper, scissors, markers, pencil, fabric paints or embellishments (optional).

Directions: Take a piece of fabric and draw a heart on it using a marker. Cut the heart shape out and use it as a template to make another. Put the two pieces of fabric together with the wrong sides facing out. Sew around the edge of the heart, leaving 1/3 of it unsewn. Turn the heart inside out and stuff the opening until it's half full. Take the small pieces of paper and write or draw who or what is important to you. Put the pieces of paper inside the heart before you fill it the rest of the way with stuffing. You can also add any other items that are personally meaningful. Sew the heart closed and decorate it with embellishments or paint.

Exploration:

What people, animals, places, things, or memories are meaningful and special?

What things did you add to your heart and what isn't in it?

Where could you put your heart to remind you of the things that are important to you?

Relationship & Connections

What My Hands Hold

Materials: Plaster casting material (like Rigid Wrap®), petroleum jelly, scissors, embellishments, paint, paintbrushes, cup of water.

Directions: Use plaster casting material to make a cast of your hand. First, use the scissors to cut strips of the cloth. Add a thick layer of petroleum jelly to the area of your hand that is being plastered. Position your hand in a way that feels like it represents you. Then, dip the pieces of plaster cloth into the water and wipe off the excess with your fingers. Add the plaster cloth to the bottom, top, or side of your hand but do NOT wrap your entire hand. Allow it to harden and gently remove your hand. After it has dried, paint the sculpture and add images or words that represent what's important to you.

Exploration:

Why did you choose to put your hand in that position?

What words or images did you add and why are these important to you?

Are there any qualities or values that are important to you that you didn't add; if so, what might they be?

Relationship & Connections

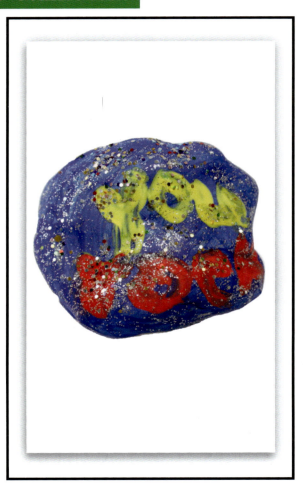

You Rock

Materials: Rock, paint, paintbrushes, decoupage medium.

Directions: With paint, add images or words to the rock that represent something important to you. Allow the rock to dry and then add a layer of decoupage.

Exploration:

Discuss what is important to you: what people, animals, places, things, or memories are meaningful to you?

What words or images are on your rock and why?

Where would you put this rock to remind you what you value?

Self-Esteem

Gratitude Tree

Materials: Large paper, colored paper, glue stick, scissors, drawing supplies.

Directions: Draw a big tree on the large paper. Using the colored paper, draw the outline of leaves. Inside of the leaves, write down things you are grateful for. Cut out the leaves, embellish them, and glue them to the tree.

Exploration:

What are you grateful for?

Are some things more important than others; if so, which ones and why?

Is there something that you left off the tree; if so, why?

Can you write, draw, or talk about what you are grateful for every day?

Where might you put your tree to remind you of what you are grateful for?

Self-Esteem

A Not-So-Strong Animal

Materials: Modeling clay, clay tools, paint, paintbrushes.

Directions: Use the clay and tools to sculpt an animal that is the opposite of strong. Allow the clay to dry and then paint it.

Exploration:

What does the opposite of strong mean to you?

What would that animal be thinking, doing, or acting like?

What are the differences and similarities between being not-so-strong on the inside and outside? How are you similar to or different from this animal?

When might you want to act like that animal?

Self-Esteem

A Strong Animal

Materials: Modeling clay, clay tools, paint, paintbrushes.

Directions: Use the clay and tools to sculpt an animal that is strong. Allow the clay to dry and then paint it.

Exploration:

What makes an animal strong?

What would that animal be thinking, doing, or acting like to show you it is strong?

What are the differences between being strong on the inside and outside?

How are you similar to or different from this animal?

When might you want to act like that animal?

Self-Esteem

Affirmation Card Deck

Materials: Index cards or slips of paper, drawing supplies, magazines, scissors, glue.

Directions: Write down positive statements and draw images or symbols that help you remember positive thoughts.

Exploration:

When throughout the day might you need a positive reminder?

Are there places, like your backpack, where you might want to leave a card?

Is there someone you would like to give a card to; if so, who and which card?

How did it feel to write down positive affirmations to uplift yourself?

Self-Esteem

Confidence Companion

Materials: Paper, drawing supplies.

Directions: Draw a character that is confident and able to handle difficult challenges. Add any special powers they might have or inspirational quotes to help you when you are feeling challenged.

Exploration:

What does this companion use to help them with challenges?

How might they act and think when they are faced with a challenge?

How are you similar to or different from this character?

What might happen if you acted or thought like this character?

Self-Esteem

Mirror, Mirror

Materials: Compact mirror, dry erase or permanent markers, embellishments, modeling or air-dry clay, clay tools, paint, paintbrushes, glue.

Directions: Use the markers to write positive words or images on the mirror. Use the clay to create positive symbols to add to the mirror and paint these after they dry. Glue the symbols and embellishments inside the compact after the paint has dried.

Exploration:

How can your "mirror, mirror" remind you to practice positive self-talk?

What are some words or symbols you can add to the mirror to help remind you that you are good enough, kind, lovable, and worthy?

What might you add to the compact to remind you to think or do positive things?

Self-Esteem

My Ideal Self

Materials: Paper, magazines, glue, scissors, drawing supplies.

Directions: Think about what you like and dislike about yourself. These can be external traits, such as how you look and what you like doing, or internal qualities, such as your beliefs or values. Now imagine your ideal self: you at your very best. Use words or images to create a picture of your ideal self.

Exploration:

What does your ideal self look like?

What would you be doing, thinking, and feeling?

What would be important to you?

Are there things you can do now that would help you to get closer to your ideal self?

Self-Esteem

Power Cubes

Materials: Modeling clay, clay tools, markers, paint, paintbrushes.

Directions: Use the clay and make a flat circle the size of a small pancake for the base of the pot. Take the clay and make a medium-sized coil and slightly flatten it. Add the coil and continue to repeat the process. You can also use markers or paint to add color to your pot. Make several cubes from the clay as well. Then, use the markers to write positive reminders on the cubes to help you when you are feeling stressed out, upset, or overwhelmed.

Exploration:

What are some of your unique qualities?

What are some of the positive reminders you wrote down to help you feel calmer?

How could these cubes help you to see a different perspective?

Self-Esteem

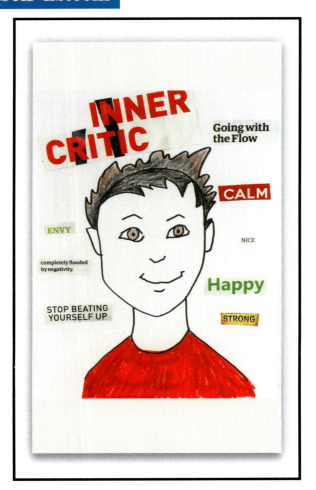

Selfie Talk

Materials: Paper, scissors, drawing supplies.

Directions: Use the paper to create an image of yourself. The image can be your full body or just your head and shoulders. When you have completed your "selfie" write down what critical things you think or say about yourself on the left side of the paper. On the right side of the paper, write down positive things that you think about yourself and positive words others say about you.

Exploration:

Were your internal words mostly positive or negative?

Were the words on the right side mostly your thoughts or what others say about you?

Overall, were there more positive or critical words on the page?

If you had a friend who said critical things about themselves like this, what might you say to them?

Self-Esteem

Shine Your Light

Materials: Glass candle holder, glass paint, paintbrushes.

Directions: Use the paint to create words or images on the outside of the glass candle holder that represent you at your best, shining your unique light.

Exploration:

When you think about your unique qualities, what makes you special?

What positive things do your parents, teachers, or friends say about you?

When you are doing things that you like or using your unique gifts, how do you feel?

How does your light shine?

Responsibility

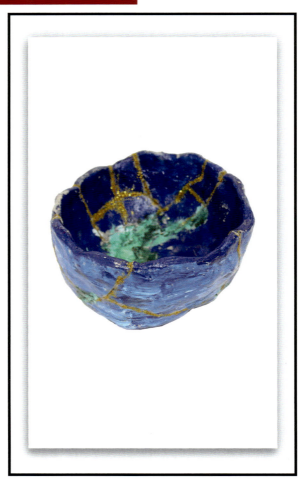

Broken But Beautiful

Materials: Pottery clay, clay tools, cup of water, glue, acrylic paint, paintbrushes, paper towels, plastic bag, gold glitter glue or gold paint, decoupage medium.

Directions: The Japanese art of Kintsugi involves fixing broken pottery with gold to emphasize the beauty of imperfections. Shape the clay into a bowl using the tools and water. Allow the bowl to fully dry and then wrap it in a paper towel and put it in a plastic bag. Hold the plastic bag above a hard surface and drop it. Reassemble the broken pieces using glue and fill in any gaps with wet clay. Allow the bowl to dry and then paint the cracks with gold paint or glitter glue. When the paint dries, coat the bowl with the decoupage.

Exploration:

When have you felt hurt or broken?

How did you handle the situation? What was helpful?

What if you saw your challenges as something beautiful, how might that change your thoughts or feelings?

Responsibility

Call the Dog

Materials: Paper, drawing supplies.

Directions: Your mind is busy and sometimes can get easily distracted with what's around you or your own imagination. Think about a puppy and how they are easily distracted yet as they grow, they can be trained to come, sit, and stay. You can teach your mind to do the same when you become distracted. Create a picture of a dog and write down any commands you might give the dog to help it remember to focus.

Exploration:

What could you say or do to remind your dog (mind) to come back to you when you are distracted?

What happens when your dog (mind) wanders and you are at school, talking with your parents, or talking with your friends?

Where could you put your drawing to remind you to focus when your mind is wandering?

Responsibility

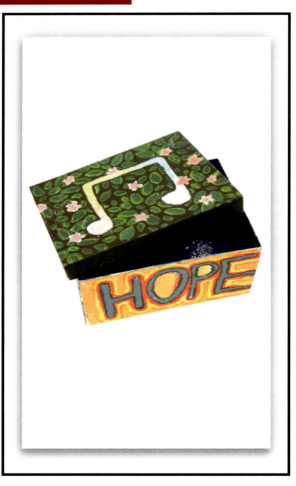

Chill-Out Box

Materials: Box, embellishments, slips of paper, markers, glue, paint, paintbrushes.

Directions: Paint the box and use glue to add additional embellishments. Use the small slips of paper and markers to write down or draw pictures of different things you can do to calm down when you are upset. Add the slips of paper along with any additional calming items to the box.

Exploration:

Which of your senses do you rely on the most to help you calm down?

When might you get triggered and need to use your box?

What can we add to this box to remind you to take a break when you are feeling upset?

Responsibility

Do-Over

Materials: Paper, drawing supplies.

Directions: Think of a challenging problem related to therapy or in general that you have encountered. Draw cartoon boxes on the paper and turn the problem into a cartoon. Then, draw another set of boxes and create a solution to the problem.

Exploration:

How did you solve this problem?

Could you have solved it in a different way?

What ideas might not be so helpful?

What might be the consequences if you made some of the choices you are thinking about?

Responsibility

I-Got-This Book

Materials: Hardcover book, paint, paintbrushes, markers, magazines, glue, decoupage medium.

Directions: Paint pages of the book and when the paint dries add words or images of things you can do to calm yourself down when you are feeling fearful, upset, or panicked. Allow the book to dry and cover it with decoupage to seal the paint.

Exploration:

What images and words can you add to your book to help you feel calmer?

When might you want to add to or look at this book?

When you are upset and overwhelmed what do you typically do?

Are these actions helpful; if not, what could you do instead?

Responsibility

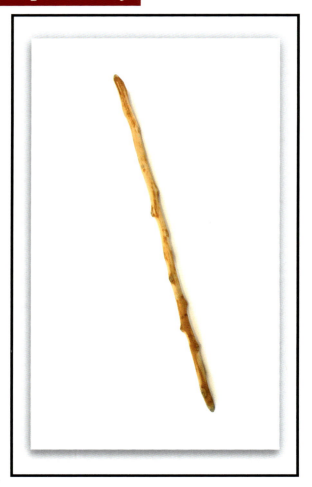

Magic Wand

Materials: Small tree branch, heavy-and fine-grit sandpaper, embellishments or paint (optional).

Directions: Take heavy-grit sandpaper and rub it over the branch to smooth it. When the bark is smooth, use a fine-grit sandpaper and rub it over the branch. If you would like, you can add embellishments or paint the magic wand.

Exploration:

If you had a magic wand, what would you wish for and why?

Is there something in your life that you wish could be different; if so, what would that be?

What would you be thinking, feeling, or doing if that wish came true?

Is there anything you can do to get you closer to those thoughts or feelings?

Responsibility

Self-Care Collage

Materials: Paper, magazines, glue, scissors, drawing supplies.

Directions: Use magazine images, words, or drawings to create a collage of things you can do when you are upset, stressed out, or worried.

Exploration:

When might you want to look at this collage?

When you are upset and overwhelmed, what do you typically do?

Are these actions helpful or hurtful; why?

Responsibility

Superpower

Materials: Paper, drawing supplies.

Directions: Imagine you woke up tomorrow morning and found out you had a superpower. Draw an image of you using your superpower.

Exploration:

What superpower did you choose and why would that power be helpful?

What would you be doing, thinking, and feeling to let you know that you have this power?

Would imagining you had this superpower be helpful at times; why or why not?

Control

Feelings Box

Materials: Box, paint, glitter glue, glitter, embellishments, small slips of paper, markers, glue, paintbrushes.

Directions: Paint the box and let it dry. Then, use glue to add embellishments such as feathers, gems, or pictures. Use the slips of paper and markers to write down different feelings and times when you have experienced them. Put the slips into the box and add to it when big feelings come up.

Exploration:

Sometimes feelings seem intense, scary, or overwhelming; what are some of the big feelings that you have?

What can you do when you have upsetting feelings to help you feel in control?

What are some of the positive feelings you have; what was happening that may have influenced your feelings?

Who else can you safely share your feelings with?

Control

Stress Pot

Materials: Modeling clay, clay tools, fine-tipped markers, small slips of paper.

Directions: Use the clay and make a flat circle the size of a small pancake for the base of the pot. Take the clay and make a medium-sized coil and slightly flatten it. Use the marker and write a worry on the coil and then circle it around the bottom. Continue to make coils until the pot is a couple of inches tall. On the slips of paper, write or draw different ways to cope with the worries. Add the slips after the pot has dried and pick one when you need a stress break.

Exploration:

How many stressors do you have today and how big are they?

Are the stressors bigger or smaller than they were yesterday, last week, or last month?

What made them change in size?

What might you do in the future to change the intensity of your stress?

Control

Favorite Food

Materials: Air-dry clay, clay tools, paint, paintbrushes.

Directions: Use the clay and tools to create your favorite food. Allow the sculpted food to dry and then paint it.

Exploration:

What is it about that food that makes it so good?

Think about your senses when you eat your favorite food—what does it taste, feel, or smell like?

When you eat it does it make a sound; if so, what kind of sound?

Can you take a deep breath in and smell your yummy food and then take a deep breath out?

Where can you put your food sculpture to help you to remember to breathe when you are upset?

Control

Slaying Your Dragons

Materials: Paper, drawing supplies.

Directions: Think about some things that "trigger" you; things that make you upset and feel like you might lose control, behave badly, or shut down. Draw those upsetting things as dragons.

Exploration:

What powers do your dragons have?

What do you typically do when you encounter these dragons and what might you do differently next time?

Do you want to draw a character that can stop them?

Would it be a good idea to act like that character who could slay the dragons; why or why not?

How can you slay that dragon?

Control

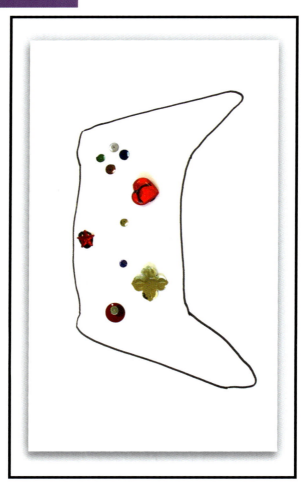

Game Controller

Materials: Paper, drawing supplies.

Directions: Think about your favorite game and how as the gamer, you can control the character's actions and choices. You are the "gamer" of your mind and you can control your thoughts, actions, and choices as well. Create a game controller on the paper and create buttons that help you with control.

Exploration:

What buttons are on your controller and what do they do?

How can you modify those buttons to help you solve challenges in your life, such as using the help button to text a friend when you feel upset?

What buttons could you add to help you feel more in control when you are challenged or upset?

Control

Being Flexible

Materials: Modeling clay, clay tools, pipe cleaners, scissors, paint, paintbrushes.

Directions: Use the clay and tools to sculpt an animal that is flexible. Using scissors, cut pipe cleaners into pieces that are a couple of inches. Insert pipe cleaners into the animal to allow the body parts to move. Let the sculpture dry and then paint it.

Exploration:

What would that animal be thinking, doing, or acting like to show you it is flexible?

Can you think of a time when you repeated the same thought or behavior? What did you repeat?

What else could you do when these thoughts or behaviors happen?

Where could you put this animal to help you to remember to be flexible?

Control

Breathing Buddies

Materials: Modeling clay, clay tools, embellishments, paint, paintbrushes.

Directions: Use the modeling clay and clay tools to sculpt a character that can help you to remember to take a deep breath when you are upset. Allow the character to dry before you paint it and add embellishments. Lie down and place your breathing buddy on your belly. See if you can get your breathing buddy to go for a rollercoaster ride by taking deep breaths in and out of your belly, allowing your buddy to rise and fall.

Exploration:

Would your breathing buddy have any magical powers; if so, what would they be?

Where could you put your breathing buddy at home?

When would you need to use it?

Control

Emotions Dice

Materials: Air-dry clay, clay tools, paint, paintbrushes.

Directions: Use the clay and tools to create a cube, like a dice. Paint images or words that represent different emotions on the different sides of the dice such as love, sadness, and anger.

Exploration:

Do you feel like your emotions are in control of you or you are in control of your emotions?

How could you feel in control?

Imagine a time when you were upset; if you rolled the dice, what other emotion might you choose instead?

Is there something that you can do or think that makes big emotions smaller?

Control

Go Slow

Materials: Modeling clay, clay tools, markers, paint, paintbrushes.

Directions: Use the clay and tools to sculpt an animal that helps you to remember to slow down and think about your choices before you act. Let the animal dry and then paint it.

Exploration:

Why did you pick this animal?

What things upset you?

What do you typically do when that happens?

What other things could you do when you are feeling upset?

Control

Intention Stick

Materials: Tree branch, paint, ribbons or yarn, scissors, glue, embellishments, paintbrushes.

Directions: An intention is often described as a goal, purpose, or plan. Add words, images, symbols, and colors to the intention stick to help you remember your goal.

Exploration:

What is your intention and why is it important to you?

What would it feel like if you achieved your goal?

What thoughts and actions will get you closer to your goal?

What obstacles might you encounter and how would you handle them?

Control

Magical Helper

Materials: Air-dry clay, clay tools, markers, paint, paintbrushes, embellishments, glue.

Directions: Use the clay and tools to sculpt a magical helper: a character that can help you solve a problem you are struggling with. Allow the clay to dry and then paint the helper. If you choose to, add embellishments with glue after the paint has dried.

Exploration:

Would the magical helper have special powers?

What would they say or do if they encountered this problem?

Would they need additional support or something special to help them?

What would they be thinking or doing after the problem has been solved?

Can you use some of the magical helper's ideas to help you solve the problem in real life?

Control

Make Your Wish Book

Materials: Decorative paper, scissors, glue, magazines, drawing supplies.

Directions: Pick decorative paper to use for the front and back cover of the book and cut it to the size of the book you'd like to create. Fold another paper back and forth like an accordion and place it inside of the covers. Then, cut off any edges that stick out farther than the cover. Glue the papers to the inside of the front and back covers and along the inside on the spine of the book. Let the glue dry. Add words, drawings, or images of your wishes to the inside and outside of the book.

Exploration:

What's your biggest wish and why?

What might you be thinking or doing if that wish came true?

What do you have control of right now that might get you closer to those thoughts and feelings?

Who might you share your wish book with; or would you prefer to keep your wishes private?

Control

Feelings Rock

Materials: Smooth rock, paint, paintbrushes.

Directions: Take the rock and make small dots with the paint around the stone and then change colors and make patterns of dots. Layer additional dots on top of the dots when the paint is dry.

Exploration:

What were you feeling before you painted the rock?

Notice your feelings after painting the rock; how does this compare to your feelings before?

When could you use this rock as a reminder that you can control the size of your feelings?

Control